D0528400

When walking through the countryside we can often see plants, animals or insects for the first time and not know what they are. Equally, we come across familiar flora and fauna but cannot remember their names. This book, with its full colour photographs and concise notes, will help you to identify these things and increase your enjoyment and appreciation of the countryside.

First Edition

© LADYBIRD BOOKS LTD MCMLXXXI

Countryside Notebook

written by Pamela K Whitehead

photographs by Michael M Whitehead

Ladybird Books Loughborough

Introduction

The countryside is a treasure trove of living things, and whether your home is there or you visit it at the weekends or on your holidays, there is always something new and exciting to see. Each different area will provide its own special interest: a plant or an insect, animal or bird, perhaps on a walk along a footpath or on an outing to your favourite wood. It is important to observe the rules of the countryside, however, and if you remember these the animals and plants you see will remain there in safety.

Birds are very shy and if you frighten them from their nests they may not come back to hatch their eggs, or their chicks could die.

Never light a fire. If it got out of control it could destroy the homes of many thousands of creatures.

The countryside is also shared by the farmer and his domesticated animals. It is as important to respect these as it is to protect the wild life, and when crossing the farmer's fields, perhaps via a footpath, do not stray and tramp across his crops. Shut gates after you have gone through them to keep the livestock in, to prevent the animals from being injured by traffic or poisoned by unsuitable food.

Litter left behind is not just ugly: it can be dangerous, especially if an animal swallows a plastic bag or treads on a broken bottle; always take it home with you. Finally, if your dog is with you, do not allow it to chase and worry livestock of any sort.

Shaggy Parasol

Late summer and autumn is the best time of year to see the brightly coloured toadstools, whose proper name is fungi, growing in woods and fields. Some of them, like the Shaggy Parasol, take their names from things that they resemble. A major part of the fungus is hidden from view, in this case below ground. The part you can see only grows so that spores can be formed and released to enable new fungi to grow from them. The Shaggy Parasol is a gill fungus, which means that its spores are held in gills below the pale brown cap.

Earth Ball ▶

A different shaped fungus which can be found on open ground is the Common Earth Ball. Unlike the gill fungus, its purple-black spores are completely enclosed in an outer skin which is covered in brown scales. As the fungus ages so this covering softens and splits, releasing clouds of spores into the air. Blown by the wind, these may travel great distances from the parent plant. Although fungi distribute many hundreds of thousands of spores each year, only a few of them will find suitable conditions in which to grow again.

Sulphur Tuft

Another gill fungus, but one that can be seen most of the year, is the Sulphur Tuft. Its bright yellow head makes it very easy to recognise, and you will normally find big groups of it on old tree stumps. Even when it looks as if it is growing on the ground this will not be so, because the roots will be in a log hidden in the earth. All fungi rely directly for their food on other plants or animals. The Sulphur Tuft feeds on decaying wood.

Ink Cap

The Ink Caps have a very different method of spreading their spores. When the fungus has matured, the cap starts to dissolve and a thick black liquid containing the spores drips on to the grass. Soon the cap will have gone completely and only the stem will be left. You will see the Ink Caps growing in groups in fields and on disturbed ground from late spring until the autumn. The liquid was once used as ink, which is how the fungus got its name.

Lichens

At first glance Lichens look like any other plants except that they may be growing on trees, as this one is, or on walls, when they are often flat and brightly coloured. They are in fact not just one plant but a mixture of two, a very simple form of green plant called an alga which is able to produce its own energy, and a fungus. The alga could live on its own, but the fungus would soon die if the alga was not present. You will find the greatest number of Lichens growing where the air is clean, away from exhaust fumes and the smoke of factories.

Bracken

Most common among the ferns is the Bracken, which goes almost unnoticed in the early spring as it forces its way through the hard earth. As the days become warmer, however, it grows rapidly as if unrolling itself, spreading its broad green leaves, which are called fronds. By summer it will have reached its full height of 1.5 to 1.8 metres, and there will be great banks of Bracken covering the woodland floor which you could walk across so easily in winter. The Bracken is a relative of the ferns which, millions of years ago, grew as large as trees.

Hart's Tongue

Ferns do not bear flowers or produce seed but grow from spores in a similar way to the fungi. The spores are contained in pockets on the underside of the leaves. This you will see clearly if you look at the pale green crinkly fronds of the Hart's Tongue Fern, which gets its name from its likeness to the tongue of the 'hart', a female deer. Look out for it in shady places on hedgebanks and in cracks in stone walls.

Coltsfoot

The bright yellow head and purple scaled stem of the Coltsfoot can be seen on bare and waste ground between February and April. Soon after the flower has formed, the white fluffy clock appears which carries the seeds for the next season. By blowing away the soft down to tell the time you are taking the place of the wind, because this is how the Coltsfoot spreads its seeds. The very big leaves remain long after the flower has disappeared. If you look at them carefully you will see how the Coltsfoot gets its name – the leaves are in the shape of a colt's or horse's hooves.

Great Bindweed

Some of the flowers to be found in the countryside do not really belong but have found their way here from other parts of the world. So it is with the Great Bindweed, which originally came from Southern Europe. The plant gets its name from its habit of binding itself around other flowers, hedges or shrubs, sometimes stunting or strangling them. This it must do because the Great Bindweed is unable to support its own weight on its very flimsy stem. The large white trumpet-shaped flowers are unscented and can be seen during the summer months.

Foxglove

As well as being one of the most beautiful of our wild flowers, the Foxglove is one of the tallest and can reach a height of 1.5 metres. The flowers are normally a pink purple, although you will sometimes find white varieties. The bees which visit the plant during the summer have to climb inside the long florets to reach the nectar, and in doing so they become covered in pollen. This plant has given us an important drug which is used to treat some human diseases.

Dog Violet

Not all flowers are as easy to see as the lofty Foxglove. Indeed, you will have to go down on your knees and search for the Dog Violet. This small plant's habit of hiding its head in the grass in the months of March to May has led to its being called the modest, or shrinking, violet. These names are sometimes given to shy people. The Dog Violet is a delicate, pretty flower with pale purple petals and deep green heart-shaped leaves. Unlike its relative, the Sweet Violet, it has no scent.

Early Purple Orchid

April to June are the months to search for one of our more common orchids, the Early Purple. Look out for its spotted leaves and deep purple coloured flower head. Never be tempted to pick wild flowers like the orchid, for many of them are rare and they have to struggle very hard to live. In their early growing period the orchids rely on a fungus to attack their roots. Only in this way can they obtain enough food to survive as seedlings.

Bittersweet

Another name for Bittersweet is Woody Nightshade, and like its cousin, Deadly Nightshade, **it is poisonous**. It has attractive berries which turn from green to a bright red as they ripen. These can be seen at the same time as the purple and yellow flowers draped over hedgerows and shrubs. The countryside is full of delicious things to eat, but there are also berries and fruit which are harmful. You should never eat anything from the countryside unless you are sure that it is safe.

Cuckoo Pint

The Cuckoo Pint, which is also called Lords and Ladies, and Wake Robin, is another poisonous plant. Seen in April, and again in August, you have probably thought of it as two separate plants. It starts off as a pale green hood shaped leaf surrounding a dark spike and finishes as a mass of orange-red berries on a stem peeking out from the hedgerow in summer. In the spring the flower gives off a strong smell which attracts flies. These become trapped, and are not released until they are covered in pollen so that they will be able to leave some on the next Cuckoo Pints they visit.

Wild Strawberry

Long before Strawberries were grown in market gardens, country folk would go out and search for them in the woods and among the grass. The fruit is also a favourite food with birds and animals which swallow the seeds as well. The seeds pass through the animal's body and are disposed of, sometimes many kilometres away from the parent plant. If they reach fertile ground the fruit will grow in following years. You can see the white flowers in April, hiding low down in the grass, and the best time to look for fruit is in July, when it ripens, but it can be found even late in the autumn.

Bramble

Bramble is another name for the familiar Blackberry which ripens during the sunny days of late summer. The soft fruit contains seeds which are spread by the many creatures that feed on the plump berries. The Bramble has another way of increasing its numbers, however. Each year it puts out long thin branches which bend away from the parent plant and root firmly into the ground. In this way, given a few years to grow undisturbed, the Bramble will spread over a large area of land. The fruit is delicious, but be careful not to eat the berries growing by the side of the road as these could be polluted by exhaust fumes from passing cars.

Hawthorn

A long time ago farmers discovered that if they planted Hawthorn around their fields, the animals could not push through and escape. This is one of the reasons why today the tree is so common in the hedgerow. It does mean, however, that every year our hedgerows are covered in thick white Hawthorn blossom. By late summer the berries will have ripened to a glossy red, and these are a favourite food with birds. Other names for the Hawthorn are Unlucky May and Bread and Cheese.

Blackthorn

Growing in the hedgerow with the Hawthorn, maybe even entangled with it, you are sure to find the Blackthorn, which gets its name from the black colouring of its bark. This shrub is one of the first to blossom, and the white flowers can be seen as early as March. The berries, which are called sloes, are black, although at first you may think that they are deep purple. This colouring is caused by a powdery dust, or bloom, covering the fruits. Be careful if you pick them: the Blackthorn, like the Hawthorn, is covered in long sharp thorns.

Scots Pine

The seeds of the Scots Pine are contained in small, tightly scaled cones which take about eighteen months to ripen. After this time the scales open and release the seeds which are scattered by the wind. Cone bearing trees are called Conifers. Most members of this family are green throughout the year as instead of losing all their leaves in autumn, the leaves are shed and replaced a few at a time in all seasons. Timber obtained from the Scots Pine is used in industry and you will see it growing in forestry plantations all over the country, as well as in a natural state.

Elm

As we have already seen with the Bindweed, things which are not native to Britain find their way here from overseas. Some are harmless, but others have caused great damage in the countryside. So it is with our Elms, many of which have been attacked by a foreign fungus carried by a bark beetle. The fungus causes heart rot and finally kills the trees. The effect is known as Dutch Elm Disease. You can see the results for yourself in the lanes and fields in summer. When all the other trees are full of leaves, the infected Elms are bare.

Oak

At seventy years of age the Oak is still a young tree. Not until all this time has passed will it bear the cup and saucer shaped acorns which are its fruit, and another few hundred years must go by before it reaches old age. The Oak you see in an open field will be shorter and bushier than the woodland one. This is because it has a lot more room to spread its branches and does not have to fight for space and sunlight with other trees growing nearby. As the daylight hours become shorter in autumn, the Oak knows it is time to shed its leaves and save its strength for the winter.

Oak Marble Gall

When looking at the Oak, you may see a small round woody ball at the base of a leaf. This is not an oddly shaped acorn but an Oak Marble Gall, which is the home of the gall wasp grub. The Gall is not produced by the insect, as you might think, but by the tree. The parent wasp bores a tiny hole into a twig to lay her eggs and the Oak, feeling itself under attack, enlarges some of its tissues and creates a swelling, or Gall, around the hole. Inside the Gall the wasp grub has shelter, food and safety, although some birds, such as the Woodpecker, will break it open to eat the young wasp.

Bloody Nosed Beetle

The Bloody Nosed Beetle is the largest of our leaf feeding Beetles which are usually thought of as pests because they can destroy crops. One member of this family is the yellow and black striped Colorado Beetle, which causes serious damage to potato fields, but luckily we do not often find it in this country. How do you think the Bloody Nosed Beetle got its name? If you pick it up, or frighten it, you would soon know because it then bleeds a red liquid. The Beetle uses this method to ward off its enemies. It has no wings so cannot escape by flying away.

Caterpillar (Peacock)

The caterpillar is one of the stages that every butterfly and moth must go through before it becomes an adult and is able to lay its own eggs. The black, spiny caterpillars of the Peacock Butterfly hatch in May and immediately begin to eat the stinging nettle leaves on which the olive green eggs were laid. They feed all the time, shedding their skins as they become too big for them. Eggs are always placed on plants which the caterpillars eat. One of the reasons why some butterflies and moths are rare is that their food supply is hard to find.

Caterpillar (Lackey)

Not all caterpillars are as harmless to man as the Peacock because many of them feed on plants which we eat ourselves. The Lackey Moth will lay its eggs on fruit trees such as the apple and plum. In April several hundred caterpillars can hatch from the eggs of just one of these moths and they will soon strip the tree of its young green leaves. The bright stripes of the caterpillar can be seen easily but it is not often attacked. Birds soon learn that the colouring means that the caterpillar is not very nice to eat.

Pupa

When fully grown, the caterpillar enters the next stage of its life. It becomes very still, maybe hanging head downwards from a leaf or twig, and the body shortens and fattens. Some of them spin a cocoon, or bag, of silk around themselves. Others use silk to anchor themselves in a safe place and the skin hardens to form a protective shell. This is known as the pupa or chrysalis. Then the biggest change of all takes place as, inside the pupa, the wings, body and head of the butterfly or moth form. Most pupae stay like this through the winter months. They are very well hidden so you will have to search hard to find them.

Small Tortoiseshell

The Small Tortoiseshell goes from full grown caterpillar to pupa and then to butterfly in two weeks. Every year two or even three generations appear, all capable of laying fifty to one hundred eggs each, so it is easy to see why this is one of our most common butterflies. When the winter comes the Small Tortoiseshell looks for a dark sheltered spot to sleep in until the warmer weather, and it is one of the first butterflies you can see in the spring.

Red Admiral

You may see many Red Admirals fluttering in the fields one year, but very few the next. This is because they do not live in this country all the time but visit us from Southern Europe in the spring. The Red Admiral is a member of the same family as the Small Tortoiseshell but only one generation of butterflies will appear each year. The caterpillars hatch during June and turn into pupae in July and August, emerging as butterflies a fortnight afterwards. Once the days become colder, in early autumn, the Red Admiral quickly departs south again.

Common Frog

Early spring is the time when Frogs make their way to ponds and streams to spawn. From the jelly-like mass of eggs emerge small tadpoles that look like fish and breathe in the same way through gills. As they grow, feeding on water plants, they develop legs and eventually lungs so that they can breathe air. Finally their tails are absorbed into their bodies and they leave the water as young Frogs, finding shelter in the damp grass. Frogs do not hunt for food but wait for the insects, worms and slugs which they eat, to come to them.

Grass Snake

Unlike the Frog which waits patiently for its meal, the Grass Snake is an active hunter. Frogs, Toads and Newts are its main food and it will search for them in the water as well as on land. The Grass Snake is the largest of the British reptiles, and although it makes a hissing noise when angry it is quite harmless. Like all snakes it sheds its skin and can eat creatures of a much larger size than at first would seem possible. This is because the bones in a snake's body are not rigidly joined, so that they can be stretched apart when food is swallowed.

Adder

Britain's only poisonous snake, the Adder, is really a very shy creature and it will not bite unless touched or trapped. You may see it sleeping on sunny banks in the hot days of summer, but at the slightest strange noise or movement it will quickly slide under cover again. As well as for defence, the venom contained in its fangs is used to kill the mice, birds and lizards which are its food. Most people, seeing an Adder for the first time, are surprised at how small it is, for the adult male does not even reach 60 centimetres — about half the size of the average Grass Snake.

Common Lizard

The colouring of the Common Lizard blends so well with the background that you will probably not see the creature unless it moves. This is called camouflage and is one of the ways in which Lizards avoid being caught and eaten. They have another way of protecting themselves, however, which is even more interesting. If an enemy catches hold of a Lizard's tail, the tail breaks off and the Lizard escapes. The attacker is left with something of a meal and the Lizard is not harmed by the loss. Eventually the tail regrows, but very unevenly.

Slow Worm

Slow Worm, Blind Worm and Deaf Adder are all names by which this creature is known. It is not slow, blind or deaf and neither is it a worm or an adder, although it is often killed because of its snakelike appearance. In fact it is a legless lizard, and completely harmless. The Slow Worm has a tiny mouth which can only eat insects and small slugs. It is even more ready than the Common Lizard to part with its tail. If you look closely at the Common Lizard and Slow Worm you will see how they are really very much alike.

Wood Pigeon

If you disturb a large grey bird from its perch and it takes off with a loud flapping of wings, you can be sure that what you have seen is a Wood Pigeon. This common British bird is found in woods, farmland and fields, where large flocks gather to feed. In the spring an untidy nest is built on the branch of a tree and two eggs are laid. Both male and female birds sit on the eggs until they hatch. This is not as many as some birds lay, but the adult Wood Pigeons can raise two or even three broods of chicks by the end of the summer.

Kestrel

The most common bird to be seen hovering silently above a hedgerow or field is the Kestrel. This is how the bird hunts for its food. Its sharp eyes will spot from a great height the movements of Vole, Mouse or large insect. Dropping like a stone from the sky, it snatches the prey up with its sharp talons and departs to a favourite post or tree to devour its meal. Although the Kestrel measures only 30 centimetres in length, it can appear much larger against the skyline than it does at rest.

Buzzard

High above open moors, fields and woodland, gliding on currents of air, the Buzzard searches the ground for its prey. Although very much bigger than the Kestrel its food is similar, but it will also swoop down on larger animals, such as the Rabbit, which the smaller birds of prey could not carry. You may see it roosting high among the trees or on a rocky outcrop where it returns to feed. The Buzzard is a common bird but shy of humans. Look out for the wedge-shaped tail when it is flying, and look out for the noisy reaction of Crows and Rooks as it passes near to their nests.

Wood Mouse

Wood Mice live mainly in hidden passages which run through the grass and undergrowth. They eat many different things, including seeds and berries, some of which they store in their burrows for the winter. You will sometimes find them near to houses or even inside, where they are not welcome. The cheeky creatures will even steal freshly sown seeds from the garden. Wood Mice are white underneath and chestnut brown on their backs. See how long their whiskers are — these help them find their way about, making up for their short-sightedness.

Bank Vole

Bank Voles can sometimes be seen during the day scuttling about the hedgerows and woods in search of roots, seeds and insects which they eat greedily. As they are active throughout the winter they do not store food in the same way as the Wood Mice. Voles are members of the family called Rodents whose front teeth are continually growing. It is only by constantly nibbling and chewing that the teeth are worn down. Many creatures hunt the Voles, including Foxes, Hawks and Owls. Can you see how different the Vole is from the Wood Mouse, even though they both have long whiskers?

Short Tailed Vole

A close relative of the Bank Vole is the Short Tailed Vole, and on first glance they look very much alike. However, as its name indicates, the Short Tailed Vole has a very short tail. It is a creature of the fields and damp pastures rather than of the banks and hedgerows, although you will sometimes find both voles in the same area. The nest of the Short Tailed Vole is very hard to find as it consists of a neatly woven ball of grass hidden low down on the ground among other plants. The Short Tailed Vole hoards quantities of food and is active during the day as well as at night.

Common Shrew

The diet of the Common Shrew consists almost entirely of insects, slugs and worms, and apart from brief periods of rest it is constantly searching for food. It pokes among the roots and dry ditches with its pointed snout, turning over leaves and small stones. Although tiny, the Shrew is very bold and will struggle with the largest worm until it is finally eaten. The young form a little procession behind the mother, each one holding on to a tail in train-like fashion as they move around from place to place.

Grey Squirrel

The Grey Squirrel is one of the few wild creatures that can be seen easily as many of them have made their homes in public parks and gardens. They came to us first from North America as zoo animals, but can now be found all over the country and are far more common than our native Red Squirrel. Squirrels spend their lives in trees. As you might expect, they are wonderful climbers and can leap easily from branch to branch in search of the nuts and pine cones on which they feed. Some of these will be stored for the winter.

Hedgehog

In the wild the Hedgehog eats many things, and like the Shrew uses its long nose to hunt for worms, snails and slugs in the earth and under leaves and stones. Winter is spent tucked safely asleep in a dry ditch or a hole in the bank, and even during the warmer months you will usually only see this creature active at night. The Hedgehog's covering of spines protects it from its enemies and its instinctive reaction to danger is to curl itself up into a tight ball.

Rabbit

You may see the Rabbit feeding on grass by the roadside as you pass in a car, or spot it nibbling at vegetables in a field while on a walk. Once it has seen you there will be a flash of white tail, which warns other Rabbits of danger, then it will vanish into the hedgerow. At one time many of our Rabbits lived in large underground tunnels known as burrows, but they now live mostly above ground. This is because some years ago a disease was introduced by man to control their numbers. The Rabbits that preferred to live above ground were less affected by the disease, and so survived in greater numbers.

Fox

During the spring and early summer Foxes live and rear their young in underground chambers known as earths. The male is called a Dog Fox, the female is a Vixen and the young are known as Cubs. Foxes venture out from their earths mainly at night in search of Rabbits, Mice and Voles or ground roosting birds. In addition to good sight and hearing, Foxes have a keen sense of smell. This makes them very hard to approach in the wild because they can smell us long before we have a chance of seeing them.

Badger

Badgers are as hard to see in the wild as Foxes. The adults spend the whole of their lives in and around one area, sleeping during the day in deep underground burrows which are known as sets. At night they venture out in search of food which consists of insects, small mammals and roots. Badgers are also very fond of sweet things and will raid wasps' and bees' nests for the honeycomb full of grubs. Their thick black and grey coats protect them from stings. This colouring also means that they can blend into the dark background at night and not be seen.

Roe Deer

The pretty little Roe Deer are native to Britain and can be found in parts of the country where there are large areas of dense woodland. The male Roe Deer is called a Buck, the female a Doe and the young are Fawns. The Buck grows small antlers, which are made of bone. Every year he sheds these and grows another pair. Like most breeds of Deer, the Bucks rival for leadership of the Does during the year and the sound of their antlers clashing together can be heard echoing through the wood. This is the mating season, known as the rut, and during this time it is best not to approach any deer as their antlers can be dangerous.

Chinese Water Deer

As its name suggests, the Chinese Water Deer comes from China, where it makes its home in the marshy areas in river valleys. It was introduced into parks in this country at the beginning of the century, but can now be found living wild in thick woodland in some counties.

The Chinese Water Deer is very unusual because it is one of only two breeds of deer in the world that do not grow antlers. What it does have, however, are long canine teeth that protrude over its lower jaw. It uses these to defend itself when attacked, and the teeth can cause great injuries.

Dartmoor Pony

You can still see Ponies living wild in parts of Britain, especially in the New Forest and on Dartmoor. The small, stocky Dartmoor Ponies are thought to be descendants of animals released in Anglo Saxon times. They are not well groomed like stable horses and have very thick shaggy coats which keep them warm through the winter spent on the open Moor.

The Foals are born in spring and spend their early months close to the mother.

INDEX